Tantric Sex Guide

BY

JASMINE WILDE

TABLE OF CONTENTS

INTRODUCTION
WHAT IS TANTRA IN GENERAL?

This is one very common question, but most of the Tantric followers avoid giving a dry and cut definition of Tantra. The word itself is Sanskrit and its root, "tan," can be translated as "extend" or "stretch." Other authors trace its origin to the word "Tantras," which is the name of the religious texts (scriptures) of the Shakti worshippers.

What is Tantra teaching us and is it still relevant today?

The Tantrism has spread throughout the East Asia along with other beliefs and has incorporated elements from the Buddhist, Bön, Sikh, Hindu, and Jain religious practices. The philosophical aspects of this ancient form of art can be quite confusing to the Westerner and even some of the scholars and the devoted Tantra followers have difficulty defining the exact meaning of Tantra. However, the method is clear as it promotes self-growth, fulfillment, and wholesome living through rediscovering our own bodies, feelings, and emotions. Once a person gets to know the practice, rituals, and the sexual rites, they can start living better and more satisfactory life.

What is Tantra and how does it fit into the Western World?

The studies of Tantra have been undertaken by many Westerners even back in the first half of the ninetieth century, but unlike the scholars who were deeply interested in the philosophical, religious, and ethical aspects of the Tantrism, the majority of the people in the West today have adopted much more simplified and practical approach. In the contemporary world, the practices are seen as a way of uniting sexuality and spirituality and often completely ignore the rituals, meditations, and the rules of behavior of the Tantrism. Despite the fact that this is criticized as a much "shallower" approach, even a basic introduction and understanding of the Tantra can be extremely beneficial for men, women, and couples.

WHAT IS TANTRA AND TANTRIC SEX?

Tantric sex is defined by the belief that spiritual and sexual should be channeled in a way that your sexual energy is "circled" around your partner and the perfect balance between both partners's energies and within each partner individually is achieved. The Tantra also teaches that in order to achieve the perfect sexual union, all barriers and blocks should be overcome. The practice is extremely beneficial for men and women alike as it teaches the former not to seek to be always in control and can help women get over certain blocks and put behind them previous negative experiences. Quite often, the Tantric sex practices, or at least some of their elements, are used in couples or individual's sex therapies and lead to better understanding of one's own and their partner's sexuality.

TANTRIC SEX - WHAT'S THE DIFFERENCE?

Here in the west, we are bombarded with false information about tantra. Authentic tantra is the union of two souls, the art and science of joining body, mind and spirit. It is the study of vibratory energies, the union of opposite polarities, the feminine and masculine conjoined in a harmonious duet of love and beauty. This yoga requires the aspirant to master and discipline his/her body and mind to illuminate the Spirit within and without. Tantra yoga can be a difficult and treacherous practice. Surrender of the ego insists upon commitment, dedication and the spirit of the warrior.

The disciplines of tantra yoga include pranayam, hatha yoga, ayurveda, jyotish, kundalini awakening, meditation and more.

-Tantra yoga is the supreme path allowing the practitioner to find heaven on earth with his/her beloved. While sex is not the focus of tantra, it is what most people want to know about when they get started. so with that in mind, let me just summarize some important facts about tantra.

-Tantra is not "free sex" or "pedestrian sex".

-Tantric sex is more than just orgasm or the union of lingam and yoni.

-Tantra is more than kama sutra positions.

-Tantra does not require toys to achieve maximum pleasure. In fact, toys are a detriment!

-Tantric sex is never boring even if you have sex every day.

-Tantric sex is never the same. It is always different and exciting.

-Tantra is not a "sport".

-Tantric sex and tantra practices have the ability to manifest siddhis, mystical powers, such as clairvoyance, clairaudience and other paranormal powers. However, we must not allow these powers distract us from our goals.

-Tantric sex is the fast path to enlightenment, meaning you can accomplish in one lifetime what would otherwise take lifetimes to do!

-Tantric sex involves the union of two people on the physical, mental, emotional and spiritual levels.

-Tantric sex bonds a couple and deepens your relationship.

-Tantric sex requires "preparation" on the part of the would-be tantric because when the powerful kundalini, sexual energy, awakens, it can overwhelm the uninitiated.

-Tantra requires a daily practice of meditation and tantra exercises to prepare you for a profound experience.

-Tantra is the sublime, mystical worship between the opposite polarities of Shiva/Shakti, yin/yang, feminine/masculine for a mutually higher purpose, that is, for their self-realization.

-Tantra can establish a seeker in a permanent state of bliss and inner peace.

-Orgasms last for 20 minutes to weeks, months and more!

-Multi-orgasms are the norm.

-Sex for 4 hours or more is normal. This isn't necessary, however it is helpful to know in order to achieve high magical states of uninterrupted ecstasy!

-Once you experience tantra, you will never settle for less! Inner peace and living in harmonious bliss is something we all dream of! That is the true essence of tantra.

THE MANY FACETS OF TANTRA

When sincere seekers ask "What is Tantra?" we might answer "like Zen, the Tao and Buddhism, Tantra is a path to enlightenment". But many modern students are stubborn and insist on a mental answer, even if it is a partial answer, which leads to the common assumption that Tantra is some kind of sexual yoga. (Isn't it?)

The favorite textbook definition of Tantra points to its Sanskrit roots. The prefix "tan" implies expansion and "tra" means liberation. Thus, Tantra can be interpreted to mean liberation through expansion. Sure, it is poetic, but it is altogether too intellectual. Tantra does not occur between the ears. Nor does it occur between the legs.

Types of Tantra

Tantra is like a wise old tree with a vast and deep root system. Some of its more developed branches include Tibetan, Hindu, Kashmiri, Shiviasm, Taoist, Kundalini, Left-Handed, Ipsalu, Quodoshka, Shamanic, Sex Magic and more. Tantra, like yoga, is not a religion. It does not exclude any portion of the human experience - it includes the full spectrum of humanity. Tantra meets people wherever they are and offers tools for them to expand. The different types of Tantra appeal to different types of people who have different needs.

Colors of Tantra

Tantra is further subdivided in terms of color: White, Pink and Red.

- White Tantra orients around subtle practices and philosophies rather than physical touch and sexual practices. They may be meditations, visualizations, higher chakra concentrations, eye gazing, breath and sound work to build sensual energy without sexual contact.

- Pink Tantra (or in some cases, Violet) embraces both the spiritual and sexual aspects of practice. This is the path where the heart is open and lovemaking is practiced with honor and reverence and healing.

- Red Tantra consists of many passionate sexual practices. Traditionally the color red connotes femininity, potency, passion and sex. This path can be liberating for the sexually repressed and may hold interest for the sexually obsessed.

Sex Magic Sexual energy is to be preserved for spiritual advancement not material gain. In the system 'Shamanic Method of Sex Magic'* the practices cultivate sexual life force for healing, pleasure and God realization. This approach is non-dualistic, releasing judgment of both material and sensual pleasures, yet is safe and heart-centered.

Neo-Tantra

Tantra may have deep roots in India and Tibet but new seeds have been planted in the West during the sexual revolution in the 1960's and 70's. The message that sexual liberation can lead to spiritual liberation is often referred to as Neo-Tantra. The most common practices of Western Tantra include balancing chakras, raising Kundalini, Goddess worship and expanded orgasmic energy.

What is Shamanism? The word Shaman means 'to know' and is the earliest known spirituality sourcing back 40,000 years ago. Shamanic practices have existed in every culture in history. Shamans have been known to:

Heal human suffering

Interpret dreams

Reverse disease

Exorcise spirits from other bodies

Channel animal guides and spiritual entities

Some of the basic tools in Tantra and Shamanism include breath, sound, movement, prayer, chanting, lovemaking and ritual. The correlation between Tantra and Shamanism is the use of ecstatic techniques to contemplate wholeness independent of religious philosophy.

In Tantra we explore polarities of male/female, giving/receiving, active/passive, self/other, mind/body, naughty/nice, duality/non-duality to lead us to greater levels of truth. In Tantra, instead of seeing the body as opposite of spirit, the body is accepted as a spiritual vessel. Sexual excitement carries with it the divine impulse for two to become one.

A BRIEF HISTORY OF TANTRA

The first question many people have about Tantra: is it all about sex? The answer is no. A small yet powerful part of Tantra's philosophy and practices deals with the understanding and cultivation of sexual energy, but it is not by any means all about sex. The second question is often: is it related to yoga? The answer is yes. In fact hatha yoga is profoundly influenced by Tantra.

Despite popular myths, Tantra isn't a crazed sex cult, a New Age fad, the Kama Sutra or even a religion. It is a philosophy and spiritual practice that began as an oral tradition and started appearing in texts in 6th century India, later thrived in Tibet and gradually made its way to the west over the past 100 years in various forms.

It's also important to note that you don't have to drop your current religion or convert to anything in order to study or practice Tantra.

While the word Tantra has several meanings, modern teachers often mistakenly believe that it means "to weave." More accurately, to spread wisdom that saves," alluding to the fact that "Tantrik practices give us a means of strengthening and protecting ourselves from worldly harm as well as bestowing the ultimate spiritual liberation." Tantra can also be translated as a "device for expanding."

To make things a little more complicated the word "tantra" can also just refer to a specific text or lineage of Tantra. So, in fact there are many tantras. I've studied a few tantras in depth: the MahamudraTantra, VijñanaBhairavaTantra, Spandakarika, as well as the lineages of Kashmir Shaivism and Sri Vidya.

While many of these classical lineages of Tantra are still studied today, most in the western world are more familiar with a modern iteration of Tantra (often called Neo-Tantra), which rarely includes classical tantric philosophy and is more focused on a spiritualization of sexuality. It's my intention to bridge these two worlds and provide a well-rounded understanding of tantric practice.

The goal of Tantra isn't how to have good sex, it's how to make life, in all its complexity (both the beauty and the pain), continually orgasmic, authentic and adventurous.

A Brief History Of Tantra

Tantra is a loose term assigned to practices characterized by ritual, rites of passage, energy work, and the utilization of the mundane to reach the supramundane and understanding the relationship between the micro and macrocosm. These aspects of Tantra can be spiritual and/or material. A guru is often consulted to help the practitioner have a mystical experience and properly guide them through the associated rituals.

Yoga is a vital part of Tantra as it awakens the ability to reach the divine in the practitioner. An integral part also of Buddhism, there is different forms of yoga in existence to meet a person's spiritual needs - varying from vigorous to peaceful movements.

Visualizations, evocations and mantras can also help the Tantra practitioner reach a point of spiritual awareness.

Tantra has had roots in areas of the world such as China, Tibet, Japan, Cambodia and Indonesia. It is closely affiliated with religions like Hinduism, Buddhism and Jainism. In Hinduism, Tantra ties closely to Vedic tradition- or rather the rejection of the orthodox beliefs. Practicing Tantra is meant to bring the practitioner a blissful feeling of self-awareness while sorting away illusions.

The exact rituals associated with Tantra are difficult to pin down since they vary greatly depending on region and the available tantric community. Commonly employed rituals include the repetition of mantras and yantras (amulets) to invoke deities. Feasts and bodily functions can also be included in the rituals. Although it gets the most attention, sexual rituals play a very small part of traditional tantric practices.

The term Tantra is of course most familiar to Westerners for the sexuality related to that small portion of rites. It is believed the sexual practices originated early in the Hindu culture as a means of forming body fluids that were thought to be transformative and a necessary offering to the deities of the Tantra. The fluid exchange often involved man, woman and guru (also a man). The female fluid was thought to be the fluid of the clan and it could be used to mark a man's belonging to that community. These rituals of Tantra evolved to focus on bliss and the divinity of union.

Tantra evolved when it moved west to become what is known as NeoTantra. The sacredness of sexuality was kept but the involvement of a guru was abandoned, as were some of the ritualistic rules and meditations. NeoTantra followers favor aspects of the Tantra like full body orgasms, the worship of the female and many do still study the non-sexual aspects of the rituals.

The history and spirituality of Tantra is so great that those merely seeking sexual thrill might want to look elsewhere. Tantric sexuality is more of a pleasurable religious act than an impulsive physical satisfaction. Studying the meaning of Tantra and employing some of the rituals in conjunction with the acts of physicality will heighten the cognitive clarity that practitioners are truly seeking. The mental effects will last much longer than the physical pleasure, but will pave the path for future enjoyments in bodily union.

YANTRA AND MANTRA TYPES AND THEIR RELATIONS

YANTRA AND MANTRA

Yantra in Sanskrit denotes a chant that will help you awaken energy by placing it anywhere in your nearby environment. Yantras tend to purify the environment and fill the atmosphere with positive energy. Yantras help our prayers reach the respective deities faster.

WHAT IS A YANTRA?

This word actually means "Loom, "Instrument or Machine." It is an interlocking matrix of geometric figures. Yantra is drawn in two dimensions and is supposed to represent a three dimensional sacred object. In short, a Yantra is a meditation tool.

A Yantra acts as a productive device for scrutiny, focus and reflection. This help us in focusing larger amounts of awareness.Yantras helps us to intensify our prayers and make our thoughts strong and influential.

Most of us cannot pronounce the mantras properly. This is when its come to our rescue. Yantras act as a strong alternative when we are unable to chant the mantras with correct pronunciation.

WHAT IS A MANTRA?

Everything around us is made of energy. Mantras are sacred sounds or vibrations that help in bringing about positivity in our lives. Mantras carry the power of changing challenges into great opportunities.

Relation BetweenYantra and Mantra

When a Yantra is worshipped properly with its co-ordinating mantras, it can fill your environment with positive energy and fulfill your desires and wishes. Yantra is a form and Mantra is the consciousness, the mind, spirit and the name of the deity. The energy in this is invoked by way of Mantras and Yantra starts showing its effect.

TYPES OF YANTRAS

There are different types of Yantras and the mantras also change according to the Yantras. There are four basic types of Yantras:

• Yantras of deities: This type of Yantra is the most significant as they are known as the ShaktaYantras or the forms of the Great Mother or the Mahavidyas. In other words, these are known as the sources of supreme knowledge

• Yantras with Astrological significance: These are used to harness the energies of the nine major planets of our horoscope.

• Architectural Yantras: These are used to evaluate the ground plans of temples

• Numerical Yantras: These comprise of a select combination of numbers which serve as talismans or charms.

Yantras, not only fulfil their fundamental purpose but also help you prosper in your career along with good health, wealth, happiness and success. These are etched in metals like silver and gold, copper and Bhojpatra which are cheaper than gemstones but are as effective as gemstones.

If they are used with proper mantras, they bring around immense positivity in your life.

Yantra Rituals

No matter which Yantra you purchase, the ritual that you need to follow is the same. However, please note that the Mantra for this will change and the Mantras need to be chanted as per the specification by the astrologer.

The ritual for performing a Yantrapooja is as follows:

• Before using the this, make sure that you purify your body and start the ritual with a positive mind.

• Start the ritual by finding a place on the floor facing the east and which is undisturbed

• You can start the ritual by lighting the incense stick and diya or lamp

• Place fresh flowers and fruits on the altar

• Place the yantra near the idol or image of your deity

• Take a leaf from any tree and sprinkle some water on yourself and then on the yantra

• Concentrate and start chanting the mantra 21 times

• Close your eyes while chanting the mantra and pray to the deity. Ask the deity to bless you with all your unfulfilled desires.

THE 3 BIGGEST MYTHS ABOUT TANTRA

If I ask you what you think of when you hear the word 'Tantra', you can be forgiven for thinking about sex.

It's a big assumption that tantra is about long sessions of sex, but in actual fact that's a myth, along with the 2 other biggest myths that tantra is about black magic of witchcraft.

Here's why...

In order to debunk the myths, we need to look at the origin and basic principle of tantra.

Originating as an Indian spirituality way back in the 500s B.C. tantra is all about connecting the individual with the universe.

If that sounds like meditation to you, then you are not wrong, because tantra does have meditation as a core element.

However, unlike some forms of meditation, which involve staring into a candle and emptying your mind of everything until there is nothing, in order to focus on the present moment, tantra works differently...

Tantra works the opposite way, by heightening your sensory awareness to hone you in on the moment which, according to the idea, will connect you to the universe.

The sexual side of tantra says that the sexual act will heighten your senses, therefore improving the tantric process, and it's this reason that sex features in tantra - tantra is not just a love making manual!

You can quite easily have a tantric moment with no sexual aspect at all, by simply focusing on your 5 senses, and what they pick up at any given moment.

The myths about black magic and witchcraft were just put about by those who were scared of the idea, who didnt like the natural expressiveness of the tantric principle.

These myths have no basis in the actual facts about tantra.

So, although the word 'tantra' conjurs up images of kinky sex or black magic ceremonies, these are just myths, and tantra is in fact an ancient spiritual idea about appreciating the moment to the full.

TANTRIC SEXUALITY - CLEARING UP THE MYTHS

In its genuine and originally intended form, tantra practice is a profound, deep and lifelong commitment. Along the way of practicing ancient tantra techniques under the tutelage of an experienced tantra teacher, the student learns to redefine his or her sexuality. However, no tantra master worth his salt will cut short the very essential process of initiation and enlightenment in order to pander to a new student's preoccupation with sex. Tantra sexuality is something to be developed in the process of spiritual evolution - it is most certainly not a feasible goal by itself.

It is natural for a student curious about tantra sexuality to ask for shortcuts from the tantra master. Popular hype has given this ancient art of love and life an unwholesome aura of eroticism. These impressions have been promulgated by self-serving charlatans who - under the guide of authentic tantra masters - seek to exploit innate craven desires. When they talk of turning you into a tantra goddess or tantra god, they obviously have no clue about what genuine tantra is all about.

Tantra is not all about sex, though sex is certainly an important channel of instruction tantra practice. It is a science that was developed to train the mind and body by harnessing unformed desires and drives into something spiritual and beautiful. Tantric sex techniques are taught only at an advanced stage of this training. Before this happens, the tantra teacher should have instructed his student in controlling the various flows of energy within the body and mind. If this has not happened, the entire process of instruction is corrupted and fruitless.

Tantric practice requires us to control and transform our physical energies, of which sexual energy is among the strongest and most predominant. While erotic pleasure is certainly a divine gift that must be accepted reverently and gratefully, we must not forget that the sexual act itself is a basic act of procreation. The central idea is that the species survives, and Nature has ensured that this happens by making it the most pleasurable act possible.

Sex should neither be vilified nor over-hyped - it should primarily be understood as a strong source of physical energy. Your tantra master will teach his students how to transform this physical energy into divine energy as well. However, this cannot happen before the student of tantra has taken a deep dive into the divine aspects of this science. Physical energy can then be transformed safely and fruitfully into spiritual energy, and the practice of tantra sex becomes possible and desirable.

The facets of ancient tantra pertaining to sexual intimacy must not be governed by base lust and carnal desire, but by a genuine desire to elevate one's partner to the status of tantra goddess or tantra god. The desire and willingness to adore and cherish one's partner as a divine manifestation is an act of worship. This worship involves rituals from which both partners benefit tremendously, both physically and spiritually.

THE WONDERFUL BENEFITS OF TANTRIC SEX

One of the objectives of Tantric sex is to take this unhappiness and turn it into a positive mindset using the body's own resources.

For many people who are over-tired or too stressed out with worries and problems are, typically, somewhat despondent about life in general and specifically are in no mood for sex. Unhappy people can also suffer from more maladies than happy people.

We can all have a lot of fun with Tantric sex. Many women are interested in Tantric sex because of the improvements to sexual health that can be harmed by the stresses and strains of modern day life and the stressful lifestyles that many of us lead today.

Men, on the other hand, enjoy Tantric sex, because it also focuses on improving erection and ejaculation. What man is not going to be interested?

Tantric sex is not just your regular "in - out - shake - it - all - about" and thank you sexual experience. In fact, true advocates who practice Tantric sex would view this as the loss of a golden opportunity to take the sexual experiences of you and your partner to a whole new level.

To quote...

"Tantric sex means taking sex to a new dimension and using it to improve the link between body and spirit and to extend the rejuvenating power of orgasm to the whole body. After all, why shouldn't we profit from something that is in our power to do, especially since it does not take much to acquire this skill?

One of the goals of Tantric sex is to stimulate the endocrine glands to produce more hGH, serotonin, DHEA and testosterone. These hormones help improve sexual health, promote the flow of blood through the body, take out the trash (toxins, that is) and strengthen the nervous and immune systems in order to increase the overall health. A person who's into Tantric sex feels healthy and rejuvenated without the use of substances or devices. Sex is quite enough to bring about these changes in a person. However, one must know how to engage in sex and what to do in bed in order to achieve this healthy state. "

This can become a wonderful self-fulfilling prophecy - improved sexual health and sexual performance also results in a huge boost in self-esteem and self-confidence, which in turn, reinforces an ongoing pattern of successful performance, improved sexual health and increased confidence, greater self-esteem. Need we say any more?

A man who can give himself and his partner a couple of strong orgasms on a regular basis is a happy and healthy man. Not to mention that his partner is also bound to enjoy a positive view on life and a general feeling of healthy living.

Practitioners of Tantric sex claim that it has a wonderful rejuvenating effect on men and women, improving their sexual health.

Frequent and powerful orgasms are a sure way of changing somebody's mood and of relieving anxiety and depression. All the maladies plaguing the modern mind (such as stress, depression, lack of confidence, and self-esteem) can be cured by having sex more often and by experiencing better and more orgasms.

Along with these problems of the mind, who knows what else could possibly be dealt with!

Through our excellent resources containing the very best in video, written and interactive sexual advice, such as our 10 Point Sex Plan, we have already ensured that bedroom blunders are a thing of the past for a number of very grateful men and their partners.

If you are keen to get sex right every time, if you are keen to bring new excitement and rekindle the fun instead of feeling the fire of doubt, then let us help you now.

Be the person you know you really want to be, you deserve it and so does your partner!

It's finally here, after years of poor quality, expensive and ultimately useless websites there is finally a program you can trust to really improve your sex life, FAST.

SEX TIPS: BENEFITS OF TANTRIC SEXUAL PERFORMANCE PRINCIPLES YOU SHOULD KNOW ABOUT

Tantra has been used for thousands of years to give people satisfaction in life. This includes sexual satisfaction. With Tantric sex tips, it is possible for any man not only to give his partner mind-blowing orgasms, but also orgasms that are long-lasting and with a heightened level of sexual pleasure. This is because Tantric sex tips usually guide a man to a new approach towards sex that ensures both great sexual performance and satisfaction. Here are some of the benefits of Tantric tips for sexual intercourse.

Tantra is all about identifying and stimulating a man's innate sensual spirituality. Through the application of these principles, one is able to enter into a new realm of sexual awareness whereby he will be able to discover parts of himself that were previously repressed. This is mainly because unlike other sex tips that usually focus on physical sexual satisfaction only, Tantra emphasizes on the connection of a man to his body and soul. As such, through Tantric techniques for sexual satisfaction, a man is able to boost his sexual performance so far as the bedroom is concerned. This sexual awareness will also be great in helping a man to last longer in bed and thus making Tantric sex tips effective tools for preventing premature ejaculation.

Sexual freedom is something that most men lack in the world today. This is mainly because of the inhibitions that people develop as they grow up. It is also because of the many

25

unresolved fears and emotional issues that men carry into the bedroom. It is therefore not a surprise that a significant number of people are having problems in their sexual lives. It is one of the leading reasons for lack of sexual satisfaction in the bedroom simply because this is why people suffer from erectile dysfunction and other anomalies such as premature ejaculation.

The meditative approach of Tantra has been refined for a long time to make sure that people, especially men, are able to enjoy and appreciate parts of themselves, especially sexual intercourse. Tantra embraces sex as a friend and doesn't treat it as a necessary evil as some people do. Sex is believed to be a gift of nature and one which should be enjoyed and explored past its limitless boundaries. One learns that sex is perfect provided that his mind, soul and body merge together with that of his partner. This usually allows for increased intimacy levels among couples and thus laying ground for great orgasms and sexual satisfaction. With increased sexual awareness and sexual freedom, the application of Tantric sexual techniques allows for the free flow of universal and sexual energy among couples. This usually ensures deeper levels of intimacy and thus great sexual performance.

Tantric Sex Improves Sexual Health

Tantric sex has a rejuvenating effect, improving men and women's sexual health.

Frequent orgasms, as one of the brain wave stimulations, will alter body chemistry. Depression and stress disappear. Women's sexual health is greatly improved. Headaches, menstrual cramps, urinary tract problems, weak immune function, incontinence, etc. virtually become a thing of the past.

In tantric sex, the brain chemistry is affected by empowering the endocrine glands for more HGH, serotonin, DHEA, and testosterone. Scientific and medical studies prove that sexual health improves drastically by stimulating blood circulation, detoxifying the body through the breath, strengthening the cardiovascular, endocrine/immune and nervous functions, leading to improved sexual health, rejuvenation and longevity.

Orgasms Strengthen Immune System

Orgasms that last at least 20 minutes can alleviate depression altogether. It could take years off our face as depression is eliminated from our life. It could prolong lifespan, strengthen the immune system, and improve overall sexual health by freeing our body and mind through tantric sex.

Men can derive great benefits by increasing sexual quantity and sexual quality in a safe, healthy, natural way through tantric sex. Tantric sex focuses on the benefits of prolonging the sex act for more intimacy and health benefits.

Sexual Issues And Concerns With Men

• Having a soft erection

• Inability to maintain an erection

• Low intensity

• Premature ejaculation

• Prolonging ejaculation

• Performance skills

• Self-confidence

• Satisfying his partner

Male sexual health

While men's sexual health concerns are more of a physical nature such as having an erectile dysfunction, women's concerns seem to be a function of their minds.

Women want to enjoy sex, but their main problem usually stems from Western-based religions or feelings of guilt and shame.

Sexual Issues And Concerns With Women

• Loss of interest in sex

• Loss of sensations

• Painful intercourse

• Inability to reach orgasm

• Having weak or mild orgasms

• Weak internal muscles due to childbirth etc.

• Sexual health concerns

• Sexual guilt and shame

• Inhibitions

• Fear of intimacy

• Need to be in control

Loss of sexual interest can arise from being too busy, overworked, having an insensitive lover who doesn't know how to make you happy. The guilt and shame factor is deeply embedded in our Western culture mainly perpetuated through religion and "osmosis" ...the Western mindset. In the East, the body and all its functions are considered beautiful and natural.

Frequent Orgasms And Women's Health

Frequent orgasms can benefit women's sexual health tremendously. However, there is a vast difference in having an ordinary orgasm and having a tantric orgasm.

Ordinary orgasms, which are the norm, are of short duration, isolated in the sex organs. Tantric sex orgasms involve the full body, mind, and spirit, lasting for hours as well.

Benefits Of Tantric Orgasm

To obtain the benefits of a tantric orgasm, the shakti, or energy, the rising kundalini, must pierce each of the chakras (vortexes of energy in the subtle body) as it ascends the spinal cord. It must reach the brain's central nervous system and endocrine command center — the hypothalamus and pituitary gland, which commands the changes that benefit our sexual health.

Benefits Of Frequent Orgasms

Frequent and powerful orgasms increase the level of the orgasm hormone, oxytocin. The oxytocin level is linked to the personality, passion, social skills and emotional quotient (EQ), all of which affects career, marriage, emotions and social life.

Orgasms are very beneficial for sexual health because they empower our pituitary (brain function).

We benefit from tantra practices on the physical, spiritual and emotional levels. Hari Om Tat Sat

UNDERSTANDING TANTRIC SEX & HOW TO ACTUALLY INCORPORATE IT INTO YOUR LIFE

What Is Tantric Sex?

Tantric sex is an ancient Eastern spiritual practice that is meant to broaden one's consciousness and to connect the polar masculine and feminine energies.

Practicing tantric sex can enable you to reach new levels of sexual energy by exposing sexual energy you never knew you had. You and your partner will undergo an intense focus of concentration that can ultimately allow you to experience hours of incredible sex, intense orgasms, and a new connection to each other, yourselves, and the outside world.

The 5,000-year-old practice of tantric sex is about enlightenment and reverence for your partner that extends far beyond an orgasm.

"In the classical sexual ritual, the participants worship each other as embodiments of deities. "We encourage people to bring an attitude of reverence into their lovemaking and to all their interactions. The tantric approach has far more to do with your mental approach than with technique. It's certainly got nothing to do with bragging about staying power."

Where Do You Begin?

It's important to understand that intercourse, not reaching orgasm, is the focus of tantric sex — they are simply possible choices on the path.

1. You begin by breathing together, moving onto making direct eye contact, and then taking turns sharing words to connect you further.

2. You then move on to lightly touching each other with your fingertips in order to awaken the nerves and heighten sensation, coming close to each other's genitals, but never quite touching them.

3. You then practice tantric kisses, in which the lips are open and the breath flows from one another freely, until finally the lips press enough to form a sensual kiss.

4. Full-body, tantric massages are next, in which one partner lies face down, while the other lightly massages non-erogenous zones for many minutes, and then moves onto the erogenous zones.

5. Sex can be the final step of this act, however it is highly advised to pick positions that make both partners feel grounded and connected, which often means keeping direct eye contact.

The Mission" of Tantric Sex

While the above steps only touch upon the practice in its entirety, they may help you to better understand that tantric sex is not a jump on and jump off type of thing. It requires time, commitment, connection, consciousness, an open mind, and so much more. It enables you to see beyond the idea of sex as something one-dimensional. And it allows you to feel the power of your partner.

1. K-Kinetic

Tantra is about "tapping into and embracing our inherent sexual energy."

2. I-Intimacy

The principles of tantra work to increase intimacy through "mindful sex."

3. S-Slow Down

As you can see from the above brief explanation of the steps involved in tantric sex, the processes of foreplay and intercourse are greatly slowed down. This allows you to be more present and pay closer attention to both your needs and feelings and those of your partner.

4. S-Sensuality

When you rev up your sensuality before you dig in to the sexual act, you allow your heart, body, and soul to open up, and in turn feel more in tune with both your own body and your partner's.

UNDERSTANDING YIN AND YANG

The Yin Yang symbol, created in ancient China, offers a complete Tantra teaching. Yin is female, cool, resting, vast, timeless, eternal, and liquid. Yang is male, hot, directional, active, dynamic, solid, and dense. In life, as in love, the qualities of Yin and Yang are in a constant interplay, weaving in and out of each other as a continual evolutionary dance. When we understand this, we no longer have to manifest a war of the sexes. We can allow the weaving of Yin and Yang elements to move and play and enjoy learning from each other through this interchange.

In the Yin Yang symbol, the black area represents Yin. The white area represents Yang. However, within the white area is a black dot. And within the black area is a white dot. This means, if you go totally into Yin it will lead you to Yang. And if you go totally into Yang, it will lead you to Yin.

The Great Life Renewing Union

This is of prime importance to understand in relation to the sexual act. For the sexual act to be completely satisfying, we need to allow equal time for Yin and Yang aspects to manifest. These aspects would like to manifest, and it is only because of conditioned beliefs around sex that we do not allow this to happen. The normal view of sexual expression is extremely limited. Two people get together and there may be a bit of genital foreplay, followed by penetration, hot active movement, and ejaculation. This scenario offers minimal fulfillment. We are capable of so much more.

In deeply fulfilling sex, there is no goal. Time stops and the way of the heart open up. No thought of performance disturbs such deep communion. There are waves of Yang, (hot activity) and waves of Yin, (stillness and melting into eternity). These waves are occurring naturally. The secret is, to just get out of your own way, and allow it to happen. When you are able to ride the waves of Yin and Yang during sex, the sex act can continue for hours. It is my recommendation, in the beginning of your experiments with this, to move into 20 minutes of Yang, followed by 20 minutes of Yin, in undulating cycles. If you can allow three cycles of Yang followed by Yin, you will have the experience of the Great Life Renewing Union, where male and female elements melt as one both within yourself and with your partner.

You will discover, as you continue experimenting with this, that your sexual compatibility is enhanced beyond anything you may have dreamed was possible. This is so, because if you give equal space for Yin and Yang expression during sex, both the man and the woman have the possibility to expand in their natural expression, which gives rise to deep fulfillment and a profound acceptance of the opposite polarity.

Practical Application of Yin Yang Principles

In general, women need 20 minutes of foreplay before penetration, meaning all over body arousal, which may include cuddling, massage, kissing, dancing, etc. Men may not realize it, but such love play is also essential for the man to relax and let go of goal and performance, and just to be with a slow build up into Yang fire. When the fire is very hot, meaning, when the man has an erection and the woman has an erection of her clitoral bulbs and vaginal lips, and is secreting copious vaginal juices, then it is a good time for penetration. Enjoy a non-goal oriented fusion of genitals, feeling and reveling in the ecstasy of Yang fire and passion. At a certain point, one or both partners may feel a subtle dip in the flow of passion. This may come with a loss of erection, or a subtle feeling of stopping. This is the signal given by nature to move into Yin.

Diving into Yin is like a small death. Remain in deep fusion either in penetration or not, but holding each other in embrace. There may be erection and penetration or not, doesn't matter. Just use this space to dive into non-doing, no movement, no sound, just melting into deep silence and restfulness together. If you had 20 minutes of Yang build up, now allow yourselves to melt into 20 minutes of Yin let-go.

Melting into Yin may feel scary, as spaces where the mind is not active appear like death for the mind and ego. However, the void space of Yin, is vitally important for fulfillment, as it is in Yin that we meet our soul and discover sources of wisdom inside which we never knew we had. It is in Yin that we are able to tap into godliness, from where all creation is born. As you melt into this space with your lover, you come back to your original oneness, the space before duality. This experience is deeply healing on all levels, bringing a most intimate and even holy quality to your union.

In some cases, the man may feel very afraid that he cannot get his erection back. Don't worry! Remember, Yin and Yang weave in and out of each other in an eternal feedback loop. When you have really let go into Yin, then automatically, after a certain time, Yang energy will begin manifesting. Like magic, your desire for hot sexual play will awaken, and the second time, you will be much more in synch with your partner as you move into Yang arousal. Once you have the knack of moving with the waves of Yin and Yang, there is no looking back. This type of sexual union is so deeply fulfilling, that it appears ludicrous to make love in the old way.

Genital Release and Conservation of Semen Practice

Of course the question may arise, "what about genital release? Is there space for genital orgasm with Yin Yang lovemaking?" Yes of course there is. On this subject, it is important to understand that people tend to go towards a goal of genital release much more often than is required by the body. As a man gets older, he needs much less ejaculation than he did in his teens for example, and to ejaculate frequently can even be detrimental to his energy levels. You can dissolve the belief that you need to ejaculate every time you make love, and this will take the pressure off. Learn to ride the waves of Yang and Yin, and as you do so, pay close attention as to whether your urge to ejaculate is coming from emotional tension or from a true physical need. Train yourself to ejaculate only when your body requires it, the frequency of which will depend on your age and health. As you conserve your semen and yet have frequent sexual interaction, you may discover that you begin a process of rejuvenation and you thing in regards to sexuality.

For a woman, the sexual response is opposite to a man. She can have multiple orgasms without loss of energy, and remains on an orgasmic plateau for at least 20 minutes after she has had an orgasm, meaning she is ready for more orgasms during that time. This is not to say she cannot benefit from relaxing around the subject of a goal during sex. It can be of tremendous benefit for a woman to also let go of the goal of orgasm, and just enjoy being in the moment with her lover, allowing what wants to unfold within the cycles of Yin and Yang. Such a deep let go can bring both the man and the woman into a deeper fusion, beyond their small selves into an orgasmic union with the whole universe.

TANTRA - YIN YANG GAZING

This is a beautiful meditation to perform before lovemaking. You can retain your yin vision while you make love. In doing so, you will allow your partner to expand into his or her full beauty and magnificence. Yin yang gazing is a way of seeing into the Buddha nature of each other—loving, quietly powerful, and infinitely wise.

- Sit opposite each other, as close as you can get with enough light to be able to see your partner's face clearly.

- Let your eyes wander naturally across the face of your partner, taking in all the details of skin, colors, and features. On how it feels to be looked into in this intense way. Both partners are in fact "receiving" the intense gaze at the same time, but don't let this distract you.

- Look at your partner's hair, neck, and ears. Allow the movement of your eyes to be free and spontaneous.

- Notice how your mind has something to say about almost everything your eyes fall upon. Don't try to hold onto these opinions - allow them to drift away as your gaze moves to the next feature, and let your thoughts follow their natural pattern without effort. Do this for five minutes. Notice how you see beauty, and how your partner transforms before you.

- Close your eyes and rest for a few minutes.

- Open your eyes again, and these times "soften" your eyes. Allow your partner to gaze into you. Receive his or her look, and let them penetrate you with their gaze. Concentrate
- After five minutes, close your eyes and rest again.

- Open your eyes and let them rest upon a point somewhere between your two faces. You will probably find yourself sinking into a deeply meditative state. Rest in the peace for a few minutes until you become alert again.

TEACHINGS

Below are some basic teachings of Tantra. These can be used to build intimacy, expand the sexual pleasure, and even transform lives and/or relationships. Used properly, they can be used to move closer to enlightenment. Each teaching may be used both sexually and non-sexually.

Breathe!

Central to most Eastern teachings about attainment of enlightenment are teachings about the breath. First off, why is this? Or, more appropriately to Tantra, how does breath relate to spiritual advancement?

We all breathe all the time. If we stop breathing for too long, we pass out or die. So in this sense, at least, breath is directly related to consciousness. Breath is energy. Each breath brings in new oxygen, which is circulated by the blood, and energizes every living cell within the body. Breath and oxygen are among of the foundations of human energy.

Most people breathe totally unconsciously most of the time. Think about that for a second. Most of the time, you don't pay any attention to your breath. It simply happens without your considering it even for a moment. Your life is entirely dependent upon something of which you are mostly unconscious.

What happens when a person makes breathing conscious? Tantra and other Eastern systems utilize breath in a conscious and deliberate manner, and thereby transform the relationship of the practitioner to their energy. By becoming conscious of the breath, and focusing intently upon it, the practitioner can move and/or regulate their energy.

If you begin to pay attention to your breath during the sexual act, or the breath of your partner, you may notice some interesting things. Very frequently in sex, when people become excited, they will hold their breath for a few moments or for a long time, then letting out or in a large amount of air. Breathing often becomes strained, or tense, and then releases suddenly. Such breathing stops the energy from moving.

In making breathing conscious during the sexual act, one may learn to move the energy at will, rather than simply allowing it to flow and stop in an unconscious manner.

The teaching here is to make the breath full and relaxed. Breathe deeply. Breathe fully. Do not stop the breath, or tighten the chest/lungs. Let the breath be complete. Full complete breaths allow the energy to move throughout the body. Short, shallow or start/stop breathing slows the energy and can even choke it off.

A more deep and full body type of orgasm becomes more easily obtainable by allowing for full complete breathing. So relax. Focus on the breath, and allow it to move completely. Feel the whole breath going all the way in and filling the lungs, and going all the way out and emptying them.

Much like the breath and the shallow start/stop breathing most people engage in during sex, muscular tension can slow the energy.

Again, for most people the level of muscular tension in the body, especially during sexual acts, tends to be a completely unconscious thing. The key in tantric energy work is to make muscular tension conscious so that one becomes intimately aware of every muscle and how it is being held. Of course, some tension is required for movement, and for holding the body up, but tension is not required for anything else.

If you make your tension conscious you may notice that you hold many muscles tense during sex with no need or purpose. If you observe your lover, he may be the passive partner during a particular sexual act, such as oral sex. He may simply be lying back and enjoying a woman's oral attentions, but still he may be tensing the muscles in his torso or legs, or any other part of the body. In such a case none of this tension is necessary, and indeed stops the flow of energy.

By simply relaxing all of the muscles not required for a particular sexual act, the energy moves through the body more smoothly and easily. Focus your attention upon relaxing all the muscles of the body. Relax. Let go. Feel your sexual energy spread into all those relaxed areas and flow throughout the body.

Relaxation, however, is not just about the body. Let go of your expectations. Let go of your preconceptions, too. Relax. Relax your rules and restrictions upon yourself and others. Release those old emotions you've been holding on to. Relax. Allow yourself to just be.

Make a Sound!

Making sound is also critical to moving of energy. Some people are nervous or self-conscious about how they sound, but do not make this a consideration in tantric lovemaking.

Let go of your internal self-talk about how you sound. Make the noises that most clearly express exactly how you are feeling right now. This type of sound may be labeled a connected sound. It is a sound connected to an emotion or sensation; the sound of whatever you are internally present to in the moment. The sounds you make will move your energy.

If you are silent, it is much harder to move your energy, than if you are very loud. The more noise you make, the higher your pleasure. The more those sounds are connected to your emotions, the more powerfully they will move the energy of those emotions.

If you attempt this, and think to yourself something like, "that emotion doesn't have a sound," or "I'm not feeling anything right now," then ask yourself these questions. What if it did have a sound? If it did, what would it sound like? What if you took that little nothing of an emotion or sensation that you're feeling right now and turned it up? What would it feel like then?

What if you spun it around, made it brighter, amplified it, and then looked again? Does it have a sound now?

If not, make one up, and keep going. If you still say to yourself, "but I don't feel anything," then ask yourself "how do I feel about not feeling anything?" This may sound redundant, but you surely must feel frustrated. Frustration has a sound too, and if it does not have a sound to you – make one up anyway.

Sometimes, we experience unpleasant or disturbing physical sensations or emotions during sex. Allow these experiences to be vocally expressed as well. Do not hold them back. If something makes you feel pain, make the sound of the pain with your voice. This not only helps to move the energy of the pain, it also is excellent feedback for your lover. If he hears you making pain noises, he can alter what he is doing to bring your noises back more towards pleasure.

Of course, you can be verbal as well as vocal. Verbal means using words. Vocal means using sounds and/or words. Feel free to outright say, that's hurting if you feel pain, or to say that's perfect, but a little more to the right if that's your truth in the present moment. Expressing through sounds, however, tends to move energy faster and more easily than expressing through words.

We can see this quite clearly in children who have just acquired language. A child of this age does not typically attempt to express emotions through language. They do it through sound. Think for a moment of a toddler in a tantrum. Typically you hear a lot of sounds, but not many words. And if words are present, they're simple and to the point, such as "NO, NO, NO, NO, NO!" Toddlers will launch their emotions off the charts at full volume, whether that calls for the sounds of laughter or the sounds of wailing sadness. Be a toddler with your expression of emotion.

Let go and really make sounds, no matter what they sound like to you or your partner, that truly express what you are physically and emotionally feeling in the moment. The more that you do this, the deeper and more connected your sex will become, and the higher you will feel as a result.

This point cannot be emphasized strongly enough. Perhaps the article should begin with sound, to stress how vitally important this component is to the practices of most tantric seekers. Of all the teachings of Tantra, people seem to struggle most with this one. Get over yourself. Open up. Express.

Make Eye Contact!

Eye contact is vital to intimacy and a deepening tantric connection. It is often said that "the eyes are the window to the soul." By connecting the eyes of two lovers, the souls communicate with each other, so to speak. Keep the eyes open, and gaze into your lover's eyes frequently. Allow the energy raised through breath, relaxation and sound to pass between your eyes and into one another. Allow the energy to pass through the eyes, and not only through the genitals.

Eye sex is fantastic, as we've all probably experienced. Think of some time you looked across a room and saw a man you were really attracted to, and your eyes met. Recall that electric, connected feeling when neither of you looked away; the desire rising in you – the power of that connection. Perhaps your heart even began beating more loudly.

Our eyes communicate in ways our words cannot. Much like sound, the energy connection is much greater when the eyes are kept connected as much as possible. In gazing into your partner's eyes, you may become aware of nuances you've never noticed before. You may see other faces in your lover's face. You may come to know what's truly deep inside by connecting in this way.

Pay Attention!

There is a saying in some tantric circles that "energy flows where attention goes." Put your attention on where you want your energy to move.

If you want a full body orgasm, put your attention on your entire body, and on feeling those powerful sexual sensations in every cell. If you want a deep vaginal orgasm, put your attention deep inside yourself, and feel those sexual sensations deep inside.

Use the breath, the muscular relaxation, the sound and the eye contact to send your focus, attention and energy exactly where you want it to go. If your attention is entirely on your genitals, this is where your sexual energy will be.

In Tantra, it is generally considered preferable to move the sexual energy throughout the entire body. To put the attention on moving the energy out from the genitals so it passes through every cell. Tantrics sometimes use that energy to revitalize the body, or sometimes for a specific purpose. Consider where your attention is during lovemaking. This is where the sexual energy will flow.

Be Present!

Underlying all of these teachings is the concept of being present. What that means is to be in the moment, not off somewhere in a fantasy, or in your mind. Be present to what is happening right now.

Many people are off in fantasy land during sex and lovemaking. They have their eyes closed, and are picturing something. Some men even deliberately picture something glaringly non-sexual and non-present just to hold off ejaculating. This is generally considered undesirable in Tantra, or any form of energy work.

By being present, a person feels more of what is happening right now, and has more energy to move. By being away during sex, it is harder to be in touch with your energy. If "energy flows where attention goes" and your attention is on a fantasy of a knight in shining armor sweeping you away, then your attention is decidedly not on your lover. Your energy will not flow to him. Your energy will flow, instead, into your fantasy. That stops the energy flow between you and your partner, and generally decreases the pleasure potential.

Final Thoughts

This write up is meant to only touch upon some elementary basics of Tantra. It is not meant to be a full guidebook on Tantra or tantric lovemaking, but to only give a taste of what is available through tantric practice.

Try using these techniques in your lovemaking, and see what comes up for you. You may find many of them far more difficult in life than they sound on paper. You may find them very easy. Check in with yourself and remain present to what your experiences are.

Conscious touch

The whole point of Tantra is to explore you and your partner's sensuality with teasing and tension - what's more sensual than touching each other?

The thing that Tantra focuses on is making each touch count, Rebecca says the key is to really be in the moment.

"If you're busy thinking about work or what you're going to eat later, then your touch will feel vacant and that doesn't feel good to anyone," she says.

We know that sometimes it's hard to really get into sex, especially if you're both busy, stressed and tired but these techniques can not only boost the quality of your sex together but your appetite for it too.

So Rebecca says forget everything and really focus on what it is you want from being with your partner.

"Be aware of where you're touching your partner and more importantly what your intention is."

Explore your senses

Tantra isn't just used to improve the physicality of sex, it's about the emotional and sensory experience too - this means taste, touch, sight, smell and sound.

"It has long been known that when we lose one of our senses, the others are heightened," says Rebecca.

By taking advantage of this idea you and your partner can experience sex on a whole other level and is why Rebecca says it is important for you and your partner to really explore each other's senses by creating an atmosphere that ignites each one.

"Create a relaxing, intimate and sensual experience for your partner by blindfolding them and offering them a variety of things to stimulate their senses.

"Try essential oils, cinnamon or vanilla for smell. Play bits of music they love or read them a love poem for sound. For taste you could feed them juicy berries, bits of chocolate or let them lick honey off your finger.

"For touch, try caressing their body with bits of silk, feathers or a rose petal. Then remove their blindfold and let them see you looking at them with love and desire!"

It might sound like a lengthy process but the result will be well worth waiting for.

Full body orgasm

We don't even need to ask if you like the sound of full body orgasms, there is only one answer, so we'll let Rebecca explain.

"One way to start to learn to have full body orgasms is to practise building up erotic energy near to orgasm, and then letting it fade a bit.

Build it up again and use your breath and the power of intention to spread the energy through your body. Play with this for as long as you like," she says.

This means taking your partner to the point of orgasm orally or otherwise but never letting them go completely over the edge.

"When you finally orgasm, you should feel ripples of it in different parts of your body."

Enjoy the journey

Tantra is not just about orgasms, in fact the whole process requires you to delay if not completely abandon your orgasm to achieve a higher level of sexual awareness first.

Rebecca says that for some of us, the fun can be sucked out of getting frisky by putting too much pressure on an end result and not focusing enough on enjoying getting there.

Tantra can put the fun right back in there, we're guessing by about 100 percent.

"If you are continually only chasing after an orgasm chances are that you and your partner are bored and stuck doing the same old thing that you know works. Quit chasing the orgasm and see what else you enjoy about sex.

"Remind yourself about why you enjoy sex and what you're hoping to get out of it. Focus on and expand other areas that you and your partner love," says Rebecca.

Whether that is the closeness you like with your partner, oral sex, kissing - whatever you enjoy - then explore that and the rest will come naturally.

7 TANTRIC MASSAGE TECHNIQUES TO HEAT UP YOUR LOVE LIFE

The Touch of Love and Compassion

Massage is a great way to relieve tension, improve blood circulation, move energy around the body and sexually arouse your lover! Massage is also a mutually satisfying way of helping couples exhibit intimacy for one another. Ours is a culture starved for touch, and massage is a quick, easy means to feed this hunger. "Easy?" You may be asking yourself. Well, you don't need to be a certified massage therapist to give a great Tantric massage. The most important component of a great massage is the desire to please your lover. So, here are some suggestions.

For starters, set the mood for a romantic environment by dimming the lights, burning some candles and incense, playing your lover's favorite relaxing music and warming the room so that both of you will be comfortable. I know pretty soon you'll be making enough heat of your own, but it's always best to start at a temperature in which you are both comfortable especially since you should both be naked.

You can use scented mineral oil, massage oil or essential oils, or edible massage creams, lotions or powder. The choice is yours.

Begin with the Back Side

About two tablespoons of oil should be enough to start with. Pour the oil into your hands first and then rub your hands together so that they will be nice and warm to the touch. Then place your hands on your lover's lower back and let your hands glide up your lovers back all the way up to the neck, around the shoulders and back down, over the buttocks and the Rosebud.

The Hand Slide

Now that you've got the oil on your lover's back, begin with your hands parallel to each other and slide them down each side of the spine, massaging all the way down to the lower back and over the buttocks. Move your hands up all the way to the neck, over the shoulders and down the arms to the fingertips. Repeat this motion at least six times. As you do this, ask your lover for feedback. If he/she is not the talkative type, then just know that it's better to make the massage too soft than too strong. Remember, it's all about giving as much pleasure as you can.

Pull-Ups

For variation, try alternating one hand after the other as you pull up and stroke the sides of your lover's body. Start by placing both of your hands over one of your lover's hips and then gently pull up towards the spine.

Move your hands to the waist and pull up towards the spine. Then take your hands to the side of the chest or breast and pull up towards the spine. Put your hands just under the armpits and pull up towards the spine. Don't forget to do both sides.

Kneading

If you have ever kneaded pizza or bread dough, then this technique will be a breeze but if you haven't, try squeezing your lover's back and buttocks between your thumb and fingers in a flowing motion (not too hard) with one hand, and then with the other hand. Now slide your hands to another area on the back and repeat until your lover has been well kneaded from neck to buttocks. The fleshy parts of the body like the buttocks can stand more pressure, so feel free to squeeze just a little harder and gently spread the cheeks as you knead. This can be very exciting for the receiver.

Feather Stroke

Before you move onto the thighs, caress your lover's neck, shoulders, arms, back and buttocks with your fingertips in a very light feather stroke for at least five minutes. If you have fingernails, gently scratch your lover with them. You can do this in circular motions, long fluid motions or from side to side. Let your light, tickly strokes and caresses create sensual anticipation for your lover as he/she won't know where you are going to tickle, scratch or touch next. If you have medium to long hair and you don't mind getting oil in it, then I highly recommend you use your hair to caress your lover's body. It is very erotic and highly memorable.

Foot Caress

You'll probably need more oil now so don't forget to put it in your hands first, then onto your lover's body.

Now do the hand slide technique on the thigh and calf in slow motion. Follow this with the kneading stroke and then the feathery one. Do one leg at a time. The feet are a major erogenous zone so let's give those tootsies some attention! Take one foot at a time and smother it in oil, spreading it around the ankle, the heel and in between the toes. Now use the palm of your hand to slide over the bottom of your lover's foot back and forth about four times. Gently rotate every toe clockwise and counter-clockwise and finally slither your forefinger between each toe. Gently pull each toe away from the body.

Turn your Lover Over

Your lover will probably have a smile on his/her face because your massage is so relaxing and sensual. Let's continue the massage by focusing on the stomach and chest/breasts. Rub plenty of massage oil in your hands and then put your hands lightly on top of the belly button, slowly sliding them up the center of your lover's stomach and around their nipples, then back down to the belly button. Do this at least five times because it feels really good and it's moving energy around the body. Be very gentle around female breasts. The male chest can handle a firmer stroke. In fact the male chest can even handle some kneading whereas feather strokes are more appropriate and pleasurable on and around the female breasts/Pillows of Compassion. Don't forget to use your hair on your lover's body.

TANTRIC SEX POSITIONS

THE G FORCE SEX POSITION

Erotic Instructions

Lie down on your back and pull your knees close to your chest. Ask your guy to kneel in front of you, grabbing hold of your feet with his hands. Have him penetrate you, thrusting forward from his hips. Looking to add even more God-that's-good action? Put your feet on his chest and have him hold on to your hips — it'll give him extra control and let him plunge even farther.

Carnal Challenge

Why You'll Love It

You have to hand over the reins to him, but it's worth it. For those who know the power of the G-spot, the deep, intense penetration will send you spinning. And there's no reason he can't be doing double duty. The G-Force is the perfect position for him to be inside you while using his hand to stimulate your clitoris. If you can surrender your on-top status, this is one position where the Force will be with you.

ROCK A BYE BOOTY SEX POSITION

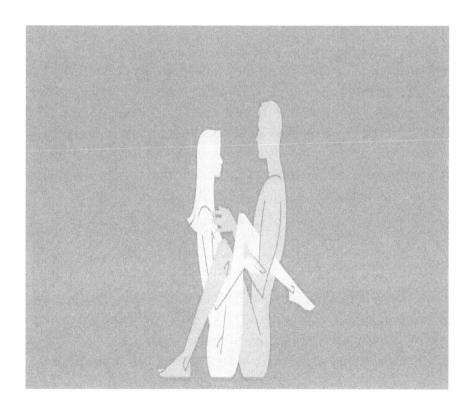

Erotic Instructions

With your man on his back, slowly straddle him. Once he's inside you, have him lift up his torso and position yourselves so that you're sitting face-to-face. Wrap your legs tightly around his buttocks and have him do the same to you. Then both you and your guy should link your elbows under the other person's knees and lift them up to chest level. Cradle each other in bear-hug fashion.

Carnal Challenge

Why You'll Love It

Even though this position limits the thrusting possibilities, you can rock each other's world by swaying back and forth. Start out slow, get the rhythm down, and then let loose. As you build momentum, keep him hard by squeezing your PC muscles — the same ones that contract when you cut off the flow of urine. This will tighten your hold on his member while increasing blood flow to your nether regions, boosting both your bliss.

Cosmo Hint

Because you and your guy are so close, this position is perfect for more intimate moments. The added face time opens up a slew of steamy smooching possibilities — so get even closer by kissing his neck or sucking on his earlobe as you move in sync.

BABY GOT BACK SEX POSITION

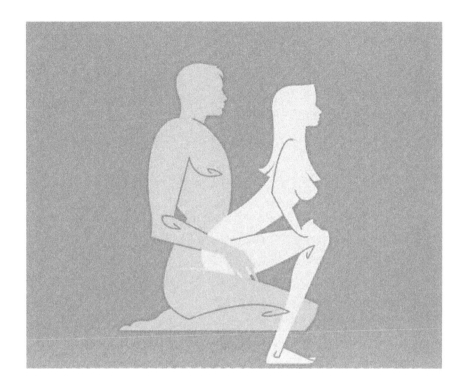

Erotic Instructions

Your best boy kneels, sitting back on his heels. With your back to him, you lower yourself onto his penis in a plié or squat, with your feet planted on either side of his legs. Placing your hands on your thighs for balance (he can place his hands on your rear for serious support), take him in only about a third of the way. Tease him for a few minutes, then gradually go deeper until you're nesting in his lap, the backs of your thighs and tush curving into him.

Carnal Challenge

Why You'll Love It

This is one hell of a chick-in-charge pose, and there's nothing like having him beg for just an inch or two more. That whimpering you'll hear is his delight as he gets a full rear view of you and feels the pleasure of long, superorgasmic strokes once you start to pump up and down.

Cosmo Hint

For maximum erotic exposure, try this in front of a mirror so you can both watch as you gradually grind your way onto his lap. There's nothing hotter than witnessing a sexy session in progress, especially when the action is all yours.

PASSION PRETZEL SEX POSITION

Erotic Instructions

Kneel face-to-face, then each of you places the opposite foot flat on the ground and nudges closer, joining genitals. Leaning forward on your planted feet, both of you lunge back and forth for a slow, upright romp.

Carnal Challenge

Why You'll Love It

This picturesque pose is the ultimate in copulatory equality: You're both in the exact same stance and share the reins when it comes to rocking each other's worlds. And since both his and your arms are available, just think of the places — backsides, testicles, breasts — they can go. While there won't be a lot of in-and-out action, your slow torso-to-torso grind provides great clitoral contact and allows a more gradual ascent to climactic cloud nine.

LAP DANCE

Erotic Instructions

Find a tall-backed chair — such as one from your kitchen table or a desk — pad it with some pillows, and sit him down. Straddle his hardened member and lean back slightly, placing your hands on his knees. Extend your legs, one at a time, until each of your ankles is resting on one of his corresponding shoulders. Pump your booty back and forth at a speed that makes you moan. To supercharge your thrusting power, balance your weight between your ankles and your hands.

Carnal Challenge

Why You'll Love It

The Lap Dance has unmatched intimacy potential — how many people have seen you this close? This primo erotic view will give your guy fantasy material for weeks to come. Spice it up with some extra-special lingerie that you can seductively toss to turn him on to add even more steam to this sack session.

TUB TANGLE SEX POSITION

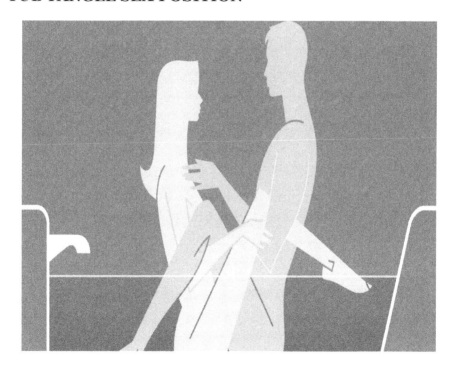

Erotic Instructions

With your man reclining in a tub full of water, straddle his lap, facing him. Once he's inside you, have him sit up so you're face-to-face. Then, wrap your legs around each other's backs and link your elbows -under each other's knees, lifting them to chest level. Hold on to each other tightly as you sway back and forth to ecstasy.

Carnal Challenge

Why You'll Love It

Talk about having a romantic romp. This position makes the most of a confined space by allowing you to entwine your bodies and create a cozy connection that's ideal for intense intimacy.

Cosmo Hint

Since your mouths are in such close proximity, indulge in lots of passionate smooching. Don't forget to nibble on tasty tidbits like his ears and neck.

TORRID TIDAL WAVE

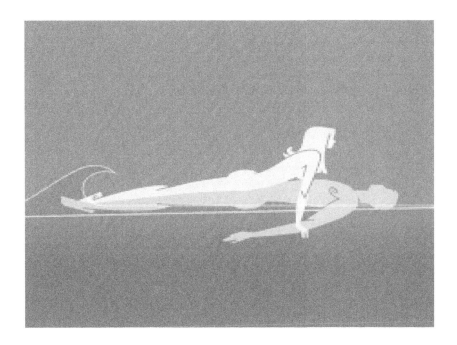

Erotic Instructions

Nothing beats this pose when you want to take a make-out session on a secluded beach to a passion plateau. Have your man lie on his back at the water's edge, keeping his legs straight and together. Straddle his penis, then slowly stretch out so you're lying right on top of him with your pelvises aligned. Lift your torso, resting your weight on your hands.

Carnal Challenge

Why You'll Love It

With every push and pull, your clitoris rubs against his pelvic bone, creating toe-clenching friction. Plus, each cascading wave sends sensation-boosting currents through every nerve ending in your skin.

Cosmo Hint

Sporadically clench your butt cheeks really tight for a few seconds so you'll be able to feel his pulsating penis inside you even more intensely.

THE SOFA SPREE EAGLE SEX POSITION

Erotic Instructions

Stand on the edge of a couch, bed, or two chairs, with your legs spread wide. Position your man so he's standing on the floor facing you. Adjust the width of your stance (bending your knees slightly if necessary) so he can easily slide between them and get your pelvises to meet — then rock your bodies together to feel the bliss.

Carnal Challenge

Why You'll Love It

There's nothing like the feeling of impulsive, must-have-it-right-now sex while standing up. But the Sofa Spread-Eagle spares you both the royal pain of matching up your private parts. While your stable stance allows you to move to his rhythm, your wide-spread legs give you that supersexy vulnerable feeling. All that frontal friction will hit your hot spot and take you to a no-hands-necessary climax.

Cosmo Hint

Because you are both standing, nothing should hold you back! Get in some hands-on action — whether you're stroking the back of his neck or tickling his testicles, he'll love the attention. Ensure you're satisfied by guiding his lips to your breasts and placing his fingers where you want them.

THE MERMAID SEX POSITION

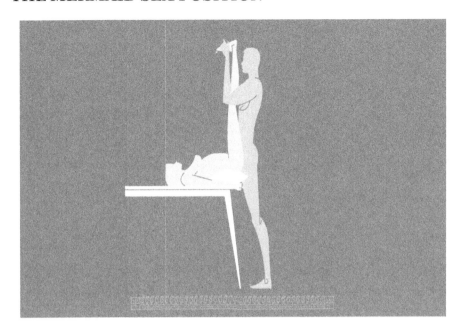

Erotic Instructions

Lie face up at the edge of a bed, desk, or countertop. Place a pillow under your butt to get some elevation. Extend your legs straight up, keeping them close together. You can put your hands under the pillow to raise your pelvis even higher, use them to hold on to the counter or desk for leverage, or keep them free. Your partner then enters you while standing up; if the bed or desk is low, he can kneel on the floor. He can grip your feet for leverage, which will give him the extra stability he needs to thrust more deeply.

Carnal Challenge

Why You'll Love It

Keeping your legs together means he feels fuller inside you, so you're creating lots of blissful friction and an incredibly tight fit. Give him a show and drive yourself wild by stimulating your clitoris while he's thrusting away.

Cosmo Hint

Occasionally separate your legs and bring them back together to get that first-tight-fit feeling again and again. The tight...tighter...tightest sensation will drive your guy wild, and the rush you'll get from calling the shots will create waves of pleasure.

THE WOW HIM POWWOW SEX POSITION

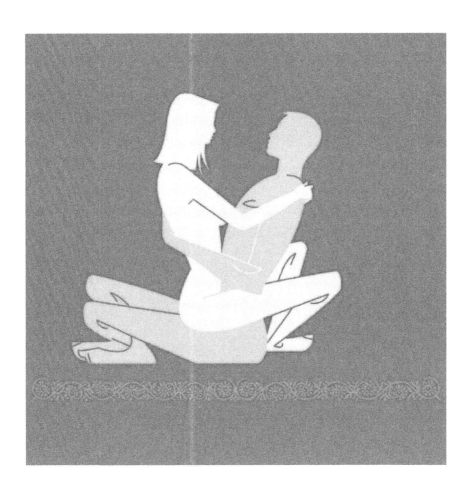

Erotic Instructions

Sit your man down with his legs crossed. Facing him, straddle his legs and lower yourself into his lap — without him penetrating you. Wrap your legs around either side of his torso, so they're hugging his buttocks. Then, as you hold each other's arms or lower backs tightly, he enters you. Start to slowly rock back and forth together, increasing your speed as you come closer to climaxing.

Carnal Challenge

Why You'll Love It

Like the standard missionary position, this takes eye contact and body-to-body closeness to the max but adds a passion perk. The comfy upright pose encourages equal control over the speed and timing of his thrusting, allowing for a gradual buildup of pleasure for both partners. Plus, your clitoris is at an easy-to-reach angle, allowing him to stroke your love button without interrupting the hot-and-heavy action.

ROW HIS BOAT SEX POSITION

Erotic Instructions

Your partner slouches down in a comfy but sturdy chair, his legs slightly spread. You straddle his lap as you face him, your knees bent and open against his chest, your feet braced against the seat of the chair. While your guy grips your hips, thighs, or butt, you clutch the back of the chair and begin moving up and down along his shaft.

Carnal Challenge

Why You'll Love It

It's traditional girl-on-top with a tempting twist. With your knees bent and your hands and feet using the chair as a springboard, it's the bounciest nooky style ever — perfect for teasing your guy with fast up-and-down action, then shifting gears and going for wide circular motions. Plus, your bodies are close enough for the intimacy of kissing, touching, or just giving each other incredibly lusty looks.

Help your partner get comfortable in the traditional lotus position, with his legs crossed and each of his heels atop the opposite knee. Facing him, sit in his lap and mount him, with your legs wrapped snugly around his waist. Embrace each other and lock lips with a shared breath, so that as you exhale your guy inhales and vice versa. As you breathe in, rock your pelvis back and tighten your vaginal muscles. As you exhale, rock your pelvis forward and release. Your guy should mirror your movements.

BASIC TANTRIC SEX TECHNIqUES

The Tantric tradition emphasizes preparation for lovemaking. Erotic rituals such as those described above focus on exchanging pleasures, awakening the senses and allowing couples to communicate on deep physical and emotional levels.

During this time, lovers are able to establish an intimate connection that can be maintained and heightened as they transition into the sexual dimension. Intimacy exercises are a form of extended foreplay, helping titillate lovers for the sex that is to come and create the optimal conditions for Tantric lovemaking.

As you experiment with Tantric techniques, don't worry whether you are doing something the "right" way. Tantra does not judge right or wrong, good or bad. Ultimately, your pleasure is what matters most.

As you transition into sex, the idea is to maintain a state of sexual ecstasy for as long as possible. Tantric lovemaking is not result-oriented, but rather, timeless and unstructured.

Maintain a deep level of intimacy. Continue to gaze into each other's eyes as much as possible. Sprinkle your lover's face, neck and shoulders with light kisses and whisper words of love and encouragement. Help each other feel loved and desired.

Keep it slow. A long, slow build helps men control orgasm and piques women's arousal. According to Tantric teacher, Robert Frey, the longer you linger in this process of building energy, the longer men can resist ejaculation. During this time, focus on each other. If your thoughts should wander, gently bring your attention back to the present, concentrating on your lover and the magic of the moment at hand.

Bring your attention back to your breath. Resist the urge to breathe quickly. Quick breathing or panting creates arousal, speeding you toward orgasm. Instead, take long, slow, deep breaths from the belly, exhaling gradually. You may match your breath to that of your partner, or try breathing alternately—as you inhale, your partner exhales. This moves energy back and forth and connects you to your lover.

Vary your positions to explore your duality. Different sex positions add to sexual pleasure and balance male and female energies. When lovers release themselves from gender roles, they are free to engage in deeper, more intimate sex. Men realize their sexual potential through surrender, by being soft and open, gentle and vulnerable. Women, in turn, can direct and initiate. As you experiment with different positions, some male-dominant, some female-dominant, explore your capacity to be strong and gentle, generous and receptive.

4 TANTRIC YOGA POSES FOR PARTNERS WHO WANT A DEEPER CONNECTION

Tantra yoga is a practice that can be used to expand the connection and awareness between a couple, creating a deeper bond spiritually with each other.

Here are some simple exercises to try with your partner. Depending on your level of flexibility, you can modify the poses. What's important is to focus on the connection and time with your partner, and enjoy each other's presence. Hopefully, you will experience an increased bond within a relaxed state. Start at your comfort level, communicate your different levels of flexibility and endurance, and most of all, practice prolonged eye contact, feeling each other's touch and positive thoughts about each other in a nonverbal way.

1. YAB YUM

This pose helps align energy between a couple. Have the larger partner sit cross-legged on a comfortable mat. Then, the smaller partner can sit on top of the other partner's thighs and cross his/her ankles behind the other partner's back. Use your abdominal and low back muscles to keep straight and aligned with each other. Bring your foreheads together, touching them gently, and breathe deeply and slowly in harmony. You can do this pose with your eyes closed or open.

2. BOAT POSE

This pose engages the core muscles (lower back and abdominals) and is a fun pose for strengthening and stretching. Face each other sitting on a comfortable floor. Reach for each other's hands outside of your legs and try to keep eye contact with each other. With bent knees, connect with each other by placing the soles of your feet against your partner's. Try straightening your legs while moving them upward, keeping the soles of your feet connected. You can modify this pose depending on your flexibility and comfort level. Focus on the touch and eye contact.

3. DANCER'S POSE

This pose focuses on balance and touch, as well as eye contact. Start standing and facing each other. Hold one of your partner's hands. Then take your other hand and reach for your ankle or shin. Bring your leg up behind you, gradually and slowly, lean your upper body towards your partner, continuing eye contact. If balance is an issue for you, you can start by having one partner perform the pose while the other holds their hand and upper arm (to assist with balance).

4. Hand-to-Heart

A wonderfully relaxing and sensual position at the end of the evening or beginning of the day is having one partner lie on their back and the other one next to them, slightly above. Look into each other's eyes. Without speaking words, keep connection with the eyes. Each of you can place the palm of your hand over your partner's heart and feel each other's heartbeat; then focus on slow and harmonious breathing. This pose is a great way to deepen the connection with each other and spend quiet time communicating without words. Switch places when you feel ready, so that each of you can experience both positions.

Tantric yoga is a spiritual and sensual way to get more deeply connected with your partner, enhancing soul attraction. Just being in the moment together with no distractions will enhance your relationship. Enjoy the moments.

TANTRIC PRACTICE: A BEAUTIFUL WAY TO MAKE LOVE

Here's one specific sacred sexual practice. Let it serve as a model for you to create your own. Adapt it in any way you wish.

+ Lie with your partner, or sit together. Bask in the beautiful simplicity of just being with each other, silently.

+ See, and enjoy, and caress each other's bodies....

+ At some time, the man says to the woman, focusing on her body, "This is the temple." At some time, the woman says to the man, focusing on his body, "This is the temple."

+ At some time, the woman focuses on the man's sacred sexual center of energy and says, "This is the key to the temple." At some time, the man focuses on the woman's sacred sexual center and says, "This is the entrance to the temple."

+ Then the key is slowly and gently placed into the entrance... and each says, in their own way, in their own time, in their own words, "We are in the temple, receiving the blessings of the Universe."

+ Words here are optional, because you may want to just go on without words.

+ Now feel, as completely and as sensitively as you can, the creative energy of the Universe flowing through you, blessing you, giving you eternal youth, eternal vitality.

+ Feel how good it is to be alive...you are life itself....

Feel your oneness with all of existence....

Feel your natural divinity....

The energy within flows from your sexual area to the highest levels of consciousness....

You are one with All....

You are light, you are life.

It is time we saw sex as the truly sacred act it is: It unites us with the forces of creation, showing us the wonder of what is. It is a true path to enlightenment.

TANTRIC PRACTICE: SUSTAINING SEXUAL ENERGY

Some men—especially young men—can find it difficult to sustain their sexual energy long enough to give their partners a truly deep and fulfilling experience. Stimulation is so intense for men that they can find it difficult to control. A few simple techniques can help give the man as much control when making love as he wishes, allowing him to reach a climax just as his partner does.

The first technique is mental; the others are physical:

1. In your mind's eye, circulate the energy through your body when making love. The intense stimulation is centered purely in your sexual center, so move the energy up your spine and circulate it around your body and your partner's body. This allows you to make love and experience sacred sex for much longer.

2. When deeply united with your partner, if the man moves more in a circular pattern than in a straight in-and-out pattern, the lovemaking will last much longer. This is more exciting for the woman, generally, and a bit less exciting for the man, giving the woman more time to catch up with the man's level of excitement and to help prolong the act of sacred sex.

Do it when you're alone. It may seem peculiar—but give it a try However, it is not recommended to anyone with a heart condition, because it is very strenuous.

1. Put your hands up over your head, and jump up and down vigorously for ten minutes while shouting, "Hu!" with force every time you land on your feet. Breathe from your diaphragm—deeply, down in your stomach, and lower.

2. After two minutes, you'll probably be exhausted. But go beyond your imaginary physical limits, and you'll find that you can jump for ten minutes quite easily, once you get into it. Don't strain, but do jump energetically.

3. Then relax.

Afterward, you'll find that the muscles in your abdominal area are much stronger, and that you have a source of power and energy within you that is much more potent than anything you might have imagined. Strenuous sit-ups would probably have the same effect.

THE IMPORTANCE OF TANTRA BREATHING

Is tantra breathing really important? If you are looking for greater sexual control, it certainly is. Tantra sex is all about mastery over one's passions, and tantra breathing techniques taught by a qualified tantric teacher can go a long way in achieving this.

The ancient yogis of India were acutely aware of the role that breath plays - not just in the sustenance of life itself, but also in the way humans respond to certain impulses. We all know that controlling our breathing in times of stress and crisis can calm our minds and help us focus. By the same coin, learning tantric breathing techniques allows students of tantra to control their sexual passion. In doing this, they become able to conserve and unleash their sexual energy at will. This kind of breathing is one of the key skill-sets that an experienced tantra teacher will bestow on his pupils.

A very significant aspect of tantric breathing is the fact that it allows the male greater control over ejaculation. By focusing on breathing at the time of greatest sexual excitement, he can withhold his body's orgasmic response - sometimes for long periods of time. The end result of such sexual control by the man is obviously enhanced erotic pleasure for himself as well as his female partner. In the same manner, the woman is better enabled to synchronize her orgasm with her male partner's if she practices tantra breathing along with him.

The ancient tantric scriptures tell us that meditating on the process of breathing during the sexual act helps the two partners to fix upon each other's tantra energy. There is a mutual exchange of life-force and erotic power. This is an extremely powerful method of bonding at the very soul level, allowing the relationship to blossom from the earth-bound to the transcendental. At the same time, the chemistry of the partners' bodies is subtly changed. There is a controlled, yet focused release of sex hormones. Also, physical energy is enhanced with the elimination of wasteful, shallow breathing and the introduction of tantric breathing.

When tantric breathing is practiced during sexual union, the quintessential tantra deities of Shiva and Shakti are locked in a celestial dance of erotic love. Their energies merge and mingle in a tantalizing act of worshipful foreplay. Their focus is totally on each other - the external world ceases to exist as they unite. This state is the very essence of tantra, and it is indispensable for those who aspire to experience the bliss of spiritual sex.

IN & OUT: BREATHING EXERCISES FOR BETTER SEX

Good sex is really simple. That's what makes it so complicated.

There are countless ways to enhance the pleasure of sex. Sexual moisturizers and introducing sex toys into the bedroom are both ways to immediately start exploring new sexual avenues. Reading erotica, watching adult films together, finding new and exciting places to make love – all of these are exhilarating ways to have better sex.

But, when it comes down to it, your body and your mind are your most important sexual assets, and there are some tricks and trips you should try if you want to improve your sexual performance. One such trick is controlling your breathing, and that's what we're looking at today.

Naked Yoga - A Celebration of the Body

Any time we engage in any physical activity, from walking up stairs to lifting weights, we need to breathe, and sex is most definitely a physical activity. The problem is, when it comes to straining through that physical activity, we tend to hold our breath. Whether we're lifting weights or having sex, we're often not breathing efficiently, and as a result our body is not working as well as it could or should be.

You ever listen to boxers, or professional weightlifters? They exhale or inhale with every effort. They condition themselves and train themselves to use their breathing to help control their muscles.

The same is absolutely true of sex: learn to use your breathing, and you learn to enjoy a new type of euphoria during sex.

And the best part is, you don't need to be a fitness fanatic or a tantra practitioner to do it (but if you've ever taken a yoga class, you're already at an advantage).

What are the Benefits of Breathing Exercises?

Consciously controlled breathing has a huge amount of benefits. For one, it can help you overcome resistance, so synchronizing your breathing with your body can quickly help ease any difficulty during, for example, anal sex, and can help make anal sex easier and more comfortable.

But it doesn't stop there. Holding your breath reduces the amount of oxygen arriving at the muscles your body is using: it makes you more tired, faster. As a result, your energy levels can dip, his erection can soften, her arousal can lessen, and the sex will end faster. Controlling your breathing will prolong sex, make him harder for longer, delay both your orgasms, and make your climax more intense when it arrives.

You know the best thing about oxygen? It gets you high. Deep breathing during sex elevates the sensation of euphoria. The more you breathe, the better you feel, and the better you feel, the better the sex.

HOW DO I TRY BREATHING EXERCISES?

1. Breathe deep &Long

We mentioned yoga earlier. In yoga, the instructor will tell you to breathe from the abdomen, using your stomach muscles to pull air down into your body. This isn't quite as simple as it sounds, and it takes practice, but it's worth it – not just for sex, but for everyday life.

2. Synchronize your breathing.

When you're making love, making a conscious effort to make your breathing patterns match is a type of intimacy exercise.

While counting during sex is far from sexy, a good pattern is to inhale slowly for five seconds, hold your breath for three seconds, exhale for seven seconds and then "observe the space at the end of the breath" – that is, pause for a couple of seconds after you've breathed out. It is of course not realistic to maintain this pattern throughout sex, but it's a good guideline, and by matching your breathing patterns with your partner's, your entire bodies will be in sync too.

3. Slow down.

As you feel yourself coming close to orgasm, slow your breathing and surf the sensations. Your breathing directly influences your climax and can control it very effectively; normally when you're close to orgasm your breathing becomes faster and shorter, you might even begin to hold your breath. The secret to edging (also called orgasm control) is being able to recognize when this is happening and breathe slower. This alone will delay your orgasm, and result in a more satisfying climax.

There we have it. Breath from your diaphragm, synchronize your breathing and slow it down when you're close. Simple, satisfying, natural and incredibly effective.

A SUPER SIMPLE GUIDE FOR TANTRIC SEX BEGINNERS

"Tantra is a set of techniques used all over the world to deepen intimacy, increase passion, and communicate in a more open and authentic way."

In a world of high stress, to-do-lists, and constantly running out of time, tantra is the perfect antidote to the routine that develops in every romantic relationship.

This beautiful art of conscious, sacred sexuality has been practiced for thousands of years by Tantric couples in order to achieve authentic love, deep and passionate connection, and Spiritual enlightenment.

And absolutely anyone today can draw from the ancient reservoir of knowledge and wisdom of our ancient ancestors!

TIP #1: Make Time For A Weekly Session

Commit to a weekly tantric session with your partner. Pick a day and time that works for both of you.

Set aside at least two hours to truly celebrate your relationship. Do not reschedule even if you're feeling tired, as your tantric session will soon invigorate your body and leave you feeling new, stronger energy flowing through you!

Be sure to stick to your special date, only rescheduling if absolutely necessary. You'll be amazed by the increased love, connection, and playfulness each session will bring both of you!

TIP #2: Be Open To Try Something New

Remember to have fun and don't take yourself too seriously. Have an open mind and open heart, even if something seems silly to you at first.

Many people who are new to tantra have declared the eye-gazing exercise awkward and weird... until they tried it!

Don't dismiss anything, just set some practices aside until you're ready to experiment with them later on. And make sure to remain playful and curious – if a practice feels good to both of you, you're on your way!

TIP #3: Set The Mood

Prepare for your lover by cleaning and adorning your bed with comfortable cushions and blankets. Create a feast for the senses with flowers, light incense sticks (or diffuse essential oils), plus a few fruits and drinks you both enjoy.

"Create a magical space by turning your bedroom into a temple of love."

Light plenty of candles – their flickering and dim light will bring magic into the space. Put on a soft, relaxing music playlist (that will play for at least 2 hours). And make sure that the temperature is just right so that both of you are comfortable.

TIP #4: Take A Cleansing & Relaxing Bath

Run a soothing bubble bath for your beloved. Light candles all over the bathroom, add soft music, spread rose petals on the floor, and pour a glass of their favorite wine.

Even better, you can join them in the bath tub!

TIP #5: Shake Your Body Alive

Re-sensitize your body and to release any tension or blockages.

Stand facing each other with feet hip width apart and slightly bent knees. Take a moment to relax from head to toe and next start shaking your entire body for at least 5 minutes – shake your arms, hands, hips, head, shoulders, legs... You'll just love the tingling and aliveness you'll experience afterwards!

This practice helps your bodies experience pleasure in a much deeper, more intense way.

TIP #6: Meditate Together

Meditate together to clear your minds and connect to your hearts. Sit down cross legged facing each other and close your eyes.

Breathe deeply – simply be together in silence until all the worries of the day are gone. This will help you both become fully present and focused on each other.

You can also play a guided meditation, meditative music, or just sit in silence.

TIP #7: Tell Your Beloved What You Love About Them

Look them lovingly in the eye, and begin each sentence with 'I really love...'.

Be true and authentic, reaching deep into your heart to express all that you appreciate about them. This is not the time for a discussion but for sharing.

To open your hearts even deeper and create more connection and intimacy, use the following phrases (and fill in the blanks):

'"My heart truly desires... ", "It brings me a lot of pleasure when you... "

Once you've finished, invite your beloved to do the same for you and thank them afterwards.

TIP #8: Look Deeply Into Each Others Eyes

Look into the eyes of your beloved: the gateway to the Soul, and ask them to do the same.

Try to eye-gaze between 5 and 15 minutes. It will feel like a long time at first until you connect on the Soul level, and this connection will feel wonderful and delicious.

To deepen the experience, synchronize your breaths so that you inhale and exhale at the same time.

TIP #9 Sit In Yab Yum Pose

This traditional tantric pose is a wonderful way to connect intimately with your beloved.

The male partner sits down cross legged, while the female sits down on top of his legs facing him (clothed or naked). Embrace each other and breathe fully together. Allow your bodies to tune in to each other; to merge together in this beautiful embrace.

Feel the love you both share, the appreciation for this special moment, and the joy of being able to celebrate your relationship!

TIP #10 Engage In A Tantric Kiss

Still sitting in the yab yum position, breathe together and imagine that you're sharing each other's breath. Then join your lips in a soft, gentle kiss.

Allow your lips to melt together in a slow sensual kiss. Relax and savour the kiss as you caress your beloved's lips with your own.

Stay completely present in the moment and immerse yourself in the sensations of closeness and intimacy.

TIP #11 Give {or Receive} a Tantric Massage

Have him (or her) lay face down, as you awaken their body to various sensations.

Softly touch their skin with flowers, fabrics, feathers, ice, hot wax, fingertips. Begin with a gentle touch, then proceed to longer, fuller. Start at non-erogenous zones (back, neck, head, hands, legs, feet), then slowly excite their sexual energy, touching their bottom, inner thighs and genitals.

Have your lover turn over, and repeat on the front of their body – awakening their skin with soft touch, then massaging their non-erogenous zones first before proceeding to their chest, nipples, inner thighs and genitals.

Keep asking for feedback and remind your beloved to relax, breathe fully, and stay present.

Note: This massage is not about orgasm, so do not try to make them come – simply enjoy giving them pleasure.

How To End Your Session

At this point, you both may decide to make love – or not. If not, simply lay in each other's embrace, and share your feelings in a soft, loving conversation.

If you do decide to make love, do not rush it. Allow the penetration to happen naturally, without any effort.

Start with slow, shallow thrusts, and remain completely aware of your bodies, your energies and particularly your genital area. Guide your consciousness to travel up and down your spine – between your heart and your genitals, and notice all the sensations in your body.

And as you start to move again, allow your genitals to connect lovingly, and melt together in a sensual, ecstatic dance.

Take your time! Tantra is not a chase to an orgasm – it's a feast of pleasure, and as long as you're both experiencing plenty of it, you're on the right track!

TANTRIC VOWS

The 14 Tantric vows (Vajrayana) are:

1. To not disparage one's Master

2. To not transgress the directives of the Buddha

3. To not express anger toward "Diamond Brothers"

4. To not abandon love of the sentient beings

5. To not abandon the Mind of Enlightenment

6. To not disparage the Doctrine of one's own, or of another's tenets

7. To not tell the secrets to immature persons

8. To not abuse the five skandhas for their nature belongs to the five Buddhas

9. To not have reservations concerning the natures intrinsically pure

10. To not have love for the wicked

11. To not apply discursive thought to the wordless natures

12. To not have belittling thoughts toward the believers

13. To not adhere to the pledges in the way they were taken

14. To not disparage women, who are the nature of insight.

SPECIAL TANTRIC TECHNIQUES

Force, as it is said in most TANTRIC texts, comes out from deep knowledge, which, in its turn proceeds from direct experience. Therefore, it is necessary to begin with the simplest techniques, and then go on gradually to the most intricate ones

Some of the training techniques appear very simple in the beginning, but they should not be passed over superficially. Each part of the Tantric techniques presented here should be performed exactly as described, in all details, even if some of them may appear unnecessary, or even not entirely "logical". The rhythm of a person's individual evolution largely depends on the ardor and perseverance in the training. Thus, some will reach faster the supreme capacity of transmuting entirely their erotic energy in psihomental force, reaching thus superior states of consciousness, extraordinary capacities (SIDDHI-s), and much improved accomplishments in the field of the daily life.

The training practices are structured according to a 3-steps model:

1.- the enhanced perception,

2.- the perfect control,

3.- the masterly direction of the force.

Out of these, the control of the sexual energy is the most important for the beginners, and should be brought to perfection; the stage of perception will interest specially those who have problems in this sphere (cases of frigidity, for instance). The direction, as last stage, represents the logical continuation of the process of control, allowing the spiritual use of this highly amplified sexual energy.

The techniques are of two kinds: individual techniques and techniques for couples. The individual techniques address to beginners, when alone. However, they should not be deemed as being themselves a goal, serving only as instruments for reaching certain accomplishments; therefore, as soon as proficiency in their practice is achieved they may, and shall be abandoned in favor of the superior Tantric techniques for couples. However, first one must reach a certain mastery in their performance, as it has been said. The above mentioned specification has several reasons,. Out of which one of the most important is that the so-called individual practices have common points with the process of masturbation, which is nowadays so much widespread in the West (to the point of vast abuse). Although modern society teaches youngsters "masturbation techniques", as well as its presumable advantages, the age-old Tantric Tradition does not share at all the same view. There are, besides the loss of energy brought about by ejaculation or explosive orgasm, a lot of other factors that indicate masturbation as a negative habit, but the discussion of these factors is too large for the possibilities of a beginners' course. Suffice it to say that it may create phenomena of partial autism, or isolation from the Reality, develops certain forms of egoism, and a certain artificiality of behaviour. Actually, as anyone will be able to note by the practice of these techniques, there is a great difference between the lone sexual training, and the outer reality – the "world" – the communion between two lovers in an effervescent sexual play.

TECHNIQUES FOR MEN

The MANTRAof awareness (perception)

The sounds: AUM AHDI AUM. Learn them, and use them only in connection with these techniques.

They may be tuned with loud voice, uttered barely audibly, or best may be repeated mentally. The YANTRA of one's own imagery, or creative imagination should accompany the MANTRA.

Awakening

"MAHAKALA looked upon the mirror-reflection of the body that KALI had given to him. And he touched gently his body, to know the sensations of pleasure that sprang from it. And KALI directed his touch, and taught him all there was to know."

You know what your body looks like, but precisely because living with it every day you may not appreciate it at its real value, of sensitive and sensual organism. TANTRA urges you to get to know your own body in the "Tantric manner", a more uninhibited method.

Stand nude in front of a large mirror. Focus your attention on your lips, and bring the index and middle fingers of your right hand to your lips. Imagine that another person is generating these sensations to you, and repeat the Awareness MANTRA once. Now bring your left hand to the nipple of the right breast. Concentrate on the form of the nipple. Realize your sensitivity.

Feel the nipple harden. After you repeat two Awareness MANTRA-s, move the hand away. Let you left arm drop to your side. Now gently stimulate your left breast with your right hand, while repeating twice the Awareness MANTRA. Now fold your hands and let them relax against the abdomen, just below the navel. Say the MANTRA. Parting your hands, slide them downward, through the pubic hair. With the index finger and thumb, encircle your penis at its base, and tighten your fingers around it while you repeat the Awareness MANTRA. Then move your hands away from the penis, without touching any other part of it. Relax the arms. This has been phase one of the technique.

Now close your eyes. Concentrate on the detailed YANTRA-image of yourself in the nude – your reflection in the mirror. If you have trouble in establishing the image, open your eyes and look again at the reflection of your body in the mirror.

Touch your lips, nipples, and penis again. Repeating the touch will help fix the image in your mind. Eyes closed, repeat the sequence. Touch your lips with the fingers, while mentally picturing that the hands touching your lips belong to someone else. Repeat the MANTRA as you do this. Then move your right hand fingers to your left breast, stimulating the nipple as before, maintaining the image of someone else's fingers touching the nipple. The sensation of pleasure will enhance as you say the MANTRA. Do the same thing with the right nipple, and then slide the hands downward, with the YANTRA of the image of someone else's fingers grasping the base of your penis, applying a slight pressure.

Now repeat the technique yet another time, with your eyes closed, but this time imagine that the hand is yours but it is touching the lips, nipples, and penis of someone else. Let your fingertips sense the soft outline on another's lips; your fingers sense the hardening of the nipples of another person's breast; your hands slide through the pubic hair; your fingers encircle the base of a penis belonging to another person – all exploring the body of someone else. This deceptively simple technique is both relaxing and stimulating. If you practice it in the morning, it will make you feel sensually alive and well all day. When repeated in the evening, it will put your body in a state of restful relaxation.